This Is What I Want to Be

Firefighter

Heather Miller

Heinemann Library
Chicago, Illinois

©2003 Reed Educational & Professional Publishing
Published by Heinemann Library,
an imprint of Reed Educational & Professional Publishing
Chicago, IL

Customer Service 888-454-2279
Visit our website at www.heinemannlibrary.com

Designed by Sue Emerson, Heinemann Library
Printed and bound in the United States by Lake Book Manufacturing, Inc.

07 06 05 04 03
10 9 8 7 6 5 4 3 2 1

Library of Congress Cataloging-in-Publication Data
Miller, Heather.
    Firefighter / Heather Miller.
        p. cm. — (This is what I want to be)
Includes index.
Summary: A simple introduction to the equipment, uniform, daily duties, and other aspects of the job of a firefighter.
    ISBN: 1-4034-0368-6 (HC), 1-4034-0590-5 (Pbk.)
    1. Fire extinction—Vocational guidance—Juvenile literature. 2. Firefighters—Juvenile literature.
    [1. Fire extinction. 2. Fire fighters. 3. Occupations.] I. Title.
TH9148.M55 2002
363.37'092—dc21

                                2001008135

Acknowledgments
The author and publishers are grateful to the following for permission to reproduce copyright material:p. 4 Doug Martin/Photo Researchers, Inc.; p. 5 Frank Siteman/Stone/Getty Images; pp. 6L, 19 Michael Heller/911 Pictures; p. 6R Scott T. Baxter/PhotoDisc; p. 7 Mark Richards/PhotoEdit; pp. 8, 22 Ken Cavanagh/Photo Researchers, Inc.; p. 9L Dorothy L. Greco/Stock Boston; p. 9R Aaron Haupt/Stock Boston; p. 10 James Smalley/Index Stock Imagery, Inc.; p. 11L Michael Newman/PhotoEdit; p. 11R Phillip Rostron/Masterfile; p. 12 Joseph Sohm/ChromoSohm, Inc./Corbis; p. 13 Kari K. Brown/ 911 Pictures; p. 14 Rhoda Sidney/PhotoEdit; pp. 15, 16R Richard Hutchings/PhotoEdit; p. 16L Richard Hutchings/Photo Researchers, Inc.; p. 17 Brett Panelli/Stone/Getty Images; p. 18 John Burke/Index Stock Imagery, Inc.; p. 20 Timothy Tonge/911 Pictures; p. 21 John A. Rizzo/PhotoDisc; p. 23 (row 1, L-R) Aaron Haupt/Stock Boston, Scott T. Baxter/ PhotoDisc, John Burke/Index Stock Imagery, Inc.; p. 23 (row 2, L-R) Ken Cavanagh/Photo Researchers, Inc., James Smalley/Index Stock Imagery, Inc., Aaron Haupt/Stock Boston; p. 23 (row 3, L-R) Dorothy L. Greco/Stock Boston, Phillip Rostron/Masterfile, Michael Newman/PhotoEdit

Cover photograph by Skip Nall/Corbis
Photo research by Scott Braut

Special thanks to our advisory panel for their help in the preparation of this book:

Eileen Day, Preschool Teacher
Chicago, IL

Ellen Dolmetsch, MLS
Wilmington, DE

Kathleen Gilbert,
Second Grade Teacher
Austin, TX

Sandra Gilbert,
Library Media Specialist
Houston, TX

Angela Leeper,
Educational Consultant
North Carolina Department
of Public Instruction
Raleigh, NC

Pam McDonald, Reading Teacher
Winter Springs, FL

Melinda Murphy,
Library Media Specialist
Houston, TX

We would also like to thank Mike Miller of the Fort Wayne, Indiana, Fire Department and Chief Dennis Gault, Assistant Director of the Chicago Fire Department Media Affairs Office, for their help in reviewing this book.

Some words are shown in bold, **like this.**
You can find them in the picture glossary on page 23.

Contents

What Do Firefighters Do?

Firefighters put out fires.

They spray water from **hoses.**

Firefighters help people who are in danger.

They save people from fires.

What Is a Firefighter's Day Like?

Firefighters keep the fire station clean.

They wash the fire trucks and roll the **hoses**.

Firefighters exercise to keep their bodies strong and healthy.

They must always be ready to fight fires.

What Do Firefighters Wear?

bunker pants

boots

Firefighters wear **turnout gear**.

Boots and **bunker pants** cover their legs.

helmet

air tank

mask

Helmets keep their heads safe
from fire.

Air tanks and masks help firefighters
breathe in a fire.

9

What Tools Do Firefighters Use?

Firefighters use **hoses** to spray water.

They hook up hoses to a **hydrant**.

They open the hydrant with
a **wrench.**

A **pumper truck** makes water
come through the hose.

Where Do Firefighters Work?

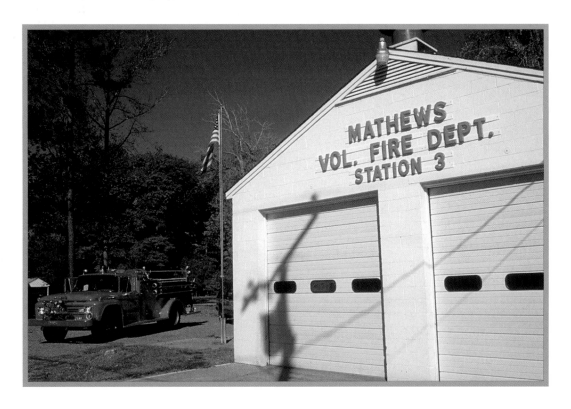

Firefighters work at fire stations.

A fire station can be large or small.

Some firefighters work in forests.

These firefighters are putting out a forest fire.

What Is Inside a Fire Station?

Fire trucks are inside fire stations.

A fire station can have more than one truck.

Some fire stations have poles.

Firefighters slide down quickly to get to the trucks.

When Do Firefighters Work?

Firefighters are at the fire station all day and night.

They eat and sleep at the fire station.

Then they go home.

More firefighters come to the fire station to work.

What Kinds of Firefighters Are There?

Rescue teams help people who are trapped.

They can use ropes and ladders to save people in high places.

The fire chief is in charge of all the firefighters.

The chief wears a white **helmet.**

How Do People Become Firefighters?

People go to special schools to become firefighters.

They read books and take tests.

They practice putting out fires.

They learn how to help people who are hurt.

Quiz

Can you remember what these things are called?

Look for the answers on page 24.

?

?

?

Picture Glossary

air tank
page 9

hose
pages 4, 6,
10, 11

rescue team
page 18

bunker pants
page 8

hydrant
page 10

turnout gear
page 8

helmet
pages 9, 19

pumper truck
page 11

wrench
page 11

Note to Parents and Teachers

Reading for information is an important part of a child's literacy development. Learning begins with a question about something. Help children think of themselves as investigators and researchers by encouraging their questions about the world around them. Each chapter in this book begins with a question. Read the question together. Look at the pictures. Talk about what you think the answer might be. Then read the text to find out if your predictions were correct. Think of other questions you could ask about the topic, and discuss where you might find the answers. Assist children in using the picture glossary and the index to practice new vocabulary and research skills.

Index

Answers to quiz on page 22

helmet

bunker pants

boots